INDIANAPOLIS

COLTS

RICHARD RAMBECK

CREATIVE C EDUCATION INC.

Published by Creative Education, Inc.
123 S. Broad Street, Mankato, Minnesota 56001

Designed by Rita Marshall
Cover illustration by Lance Hidy Associates
Photos by Allsport, Bettmann Archives, Duomo, Focus On
Sports, Sportschrome and Wide World Photos.

Library of Congress Cataloging-in-Publication Data

Rambeck, Richard.
  Indianapolis Colts/Richard Rambeck.
  p.   cm.
  ISBN 0-88682-369-2
  1. Indianapolis Colts (Football team)—History.   I. Title.
GV956.I53R36   1990
796.332′64′0977252—dc20   90-41075
                                                  CIP

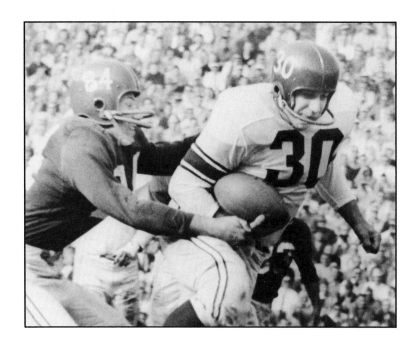

When the city of Indianapolis is mentioned, many people think of the Indianapolis 500, perhaps the most famous auto race in the world. But there's more to Indianapolis than the Indy 500. The city has more than seven-hundred thousand citizens and is the largest in the state of Indiana.

Located right in the middle of the state, Indianapolis is a city that has grown from a village of eight thousand people in 1850 to the fourteenth largest city in the United States. As Indianapolis has grown, so has the city's love of

Colts running back Alan Ameche (#30).

Defensive end Gino Marchetti joined the Colts after a superb career at the University of San Francisco.

sports. Since 1984, Indianapolis has been home to one of the most loved teams in the National Football League— the Indianapolis Colts.

Most cities, when they get a new NFL team, have to settle for an expansion franchise that has no history and no established stars. The Indianapolis fans, by contrast, got an existing team with one of the richest histories in the NFL. Robert Irsay, owner of the Colts, decided in 1984 that his franchise would be better off in Indianapolis than in Baltimore, where the team had been for thirty years.

So in the spring of 1984, moving vans appeared one evening in front of the Colts' office in Baltimore. The team's belongings were loaded into the vans, and the club moved to Indianapolis. The team brought with it three world championships and a history that included some of the greatest players in football history. Its home was now Indianapolis, but the team was still called the Colts.

UNITAS BRINGS CHAMPIONSHIP SUCCESS

The Baltimore Colts played their first season in 1953. The team was formed out of what had been the Dallas Texans in 1952. The Texans were bad, so bad that they won only one game in 1952. It would take the new Colts several years to build a winning team. But owner Carroll Rosenbloom made some very wise decisions, and the Colts started to improve.

First, Rosenbloom hired Weeb Ewbank as coach for the 1954 season. Under Ewbank, the team won more games every year. Then, before the 1956 season, the Colts gave a tryout to a young quarterback who had been drafted and

In the early 1950s the Colts were often overmatched.

1 9 5 7

Already a legend—Johnny Unitas passed for 2550 yards and twenty-four TDs during the season.

then cut by the Pittsburgh Steelers. His name was John Unitas, and giving him a tryout was one of the best things the Colts ever did.

Who was John Unitas? He was a guy the lowly Steelers had decided wasn't good enough to be one of their three quarterbacks. Unitas wrote letters to other teams in the NFL, but none was interested. Unitas wound up playing semipro ball for the Bloomfield Rams, who paid him six dollars a game. Then the Colts agreed to give him a tryout. The tryout was successful, and the Colts put Unitas on the roster. In the fourth game of the 1956 season, starting quarterback George Shaw broke his leg. Unitas was now the man in charge. He had to be, because the team had no one else. The Colts finished 5-7 in 1956, and Unitas established himself as a star of the future.

In 1958, the Colts won the Western Division title and earned the right to play the New York Giants in the NFL championship game. The Colts were heavy underdogs to the mighty Giants, but Unitas and his teammates didn't care. The Colts were a young team, and they believed they could beat anybody.

Baltimore quickly raced to a 14-3 lead, but the Giants rallied with two touchdowns and were ahead 17-14 with one minute, fifty-six seconds remaining. Unitas and the Colt offense trotted onto the field. The ball was on the Colt fourteen yard line, and nobody except the Colts and John Unitas believed Baltimore had a chance. As the New York fans prepared to celebrate a championship, Unitas went to work.

Immediately Unitas completed a pass to Lenny Moore for eleven yards. Then he zeroed in on his favorite target, receiver Raymond Berry. Bang! A completion to Berry for twenty-five yards, and the Colts were at midfield. Bang! Unitas to Berry again, and the Colts were on the New York thirty-four yard line. Bang! Berry once more, and the ball was on the thirteen. With less than ten seconds left, Ewbank sent in Steve Myhra to try to tie the game with a twenty yard field goal. Myhra's kick split the uprights. The score was 17-17. For the first time in NFL history, there would be sudden death overtime in a championship game. The first team to score would win.

1 9 5 8

Lenny Moore scored twenty-four points for the Colts in a contest with Chicago.

The Giants got the kickoff in overtime, but couldn't move the ball and punted to Baltimore. The Colts started from their own twenty yard line. Unitas used the running of fullback Alan Ameche and passes to Moore and Berry to move the Colts down the field. With the ball at the New York seven, Unitas gambled and threw to Berry, who caught it at the Giants' two yard line. After the game, reporters asked Unitas why he risked throwing an interception when the Colts were in sure field-goal range. "When you know what you're doing," Unitas said, "you don't throw interceptions."

On the next play, Ameche blasted into the end zone for a touchdown. The Colts won 23-17. They were world champions, and Johnny Unitas, the quarterback who wasn't good enough to make the Pittsburgh Steelers, was the toast of the football world. "The man was a genius," exclaimed New York middle linebacker Sam Huff. "I never saw a quarterback play any better than Johnny did in those two drives."

In 1959, the Colts won their second consecutive NFL title, beating the Giants again in the championship game,

Placekicker Raul Allegre starred for the Colts in the 1980s, (pages 10–11).

Super streak snapped! Johnny Unitas passed for touchdowns in an NFL record forty-seven straight games.

this time by a score of 31-16. Unitas was being called one of the greatest ever to play the game. He had ability and a strong arm, but what separated him from other quarterbacks was his courage.

"You can't intimidate him," said Los Angeles Rams defensive tackle Merlin Olsen. "He waits until the last possible second to release the ball, even if it means he's going to take a good lick. When he sees us coming, he knows it's going to hurt and we know it's going to hurt. But he just stands there and takes it. No other quarterback has such class.

"I swear," Olsen continued, "that when he sees you coming out of the corner of his eye, he holds that ball a split second longer than he really needs to—just to let you know he isn't afraid of any man. Then he throws it on the button."

Behind the strength of his pinpoint passing, Unitas led the Colts to winning season after winning season—although no championships—in the 1960s. In the meantime he continued to earn the respect and admiration of teammates and opponents alike.

"People talk about how brave Joe Namath is, and that's true, but he's no braver than John Unitas. No one is," stated Colt linebacker Mike Curtis. "John has broken about every rib in his body, and he has suffered jammed fingers and a broken nose and a broken elbow. Once he broke a rib and punctured his lung, and he had to have a tube inserted to drain the fluid from his lung. He played two weeks later."

Sometimes, Unitas wouldn't come out of a game, no matter what. "Against the Chicago Bears one time, my man, Doug Atkins, got through and smashed Unitas across the nose," said tackle Jim Parker. "When I came into the huddle, I almost got sick at how he looked." Center Buzz Nutter continued the story: "The ref stuck his head in the huddle and said, 'Take all the time you need, Unitas.' You know what John said to him? 'Get out of here so I can call a play.'"

When Unitas did call a play, he had plenty of weapons to use. Lenny Moore could run with the ball or catch it. Raymond Berry may have had the best hands of any receiver in the game. In addition, the Colts had a powerful tight end, John Mackey, who could run over tacklers once he caught the ball.

Sure-handed wide receiver Raymond Berry caught his 506th career pass, setting an NFL record.

On defense, the Colts had such stars as Billy Ray Smith and linebackers Don Shinnick and Dennis Gaubatz. During the 1960s, new coach Don Shula built one of the best stopping forces in football. One of the key members of that defense was a man they called "The Animal" or "Mad Dog."

CURTIS CAN'T BE TAMED, OR CONTROLLED

Mike Curtis didn't care if you called him "The Animal" or "Mad Dog." He just wanted you to know that, off the field, he was an intelligent person. But on the field, Curtis knew his job was to destroy offenses anyway he could.

Curtis was drafted by the Colts from Duke University in 1965. He soon became a starter for Baltimore as an outside linebacker. He also got a reputation as a very hard hitter. "We were playing Green Bay," said Baltimore linebacker Ted Hendricks. "Jim Grabowski was coming through the line, and Mike Curtis gave him a good old-fashioned

*Speedster Preston
Pearson averaged
over thirty yards on
kickoff returns,
including one for
102 yards!*

clothesline shot. He hit him so hard it popped his [Grabowski's] helmet off. Grabowski got up wobbly. One of our guys handed him his helmet. He started heading for our bench. I tapped him on the shoulder and turned him around and said, 'Yours is on the other side, Jim.' "

People found it hard to believe that Curtis, who was a good student at Duke, was not always the animal he was on the field. One night, Curtis and a friend went to someone's house for dinner. After the meal, the host turned to Curtis and said, "Gee, you don't act like I thought you would."

"How did you think I would act?" Curtis asked.

"Well, you know," the host answered. "You read a lot of things. . . ."

"You want me to tear up the house?" Curtis asked, surprised. "I can if you want, but it will cost you some money in repair bills."

Most of the time, Curtis did his damage on the field, and so did the Colts. They won the NFL title in 1968, with Earl Morrall replacing the injured Unitas at quarterback. But the Colts lost 16-7 in the Super Bowl to the upstart New York Jets and Joe Namath. Two years later, the Colts were in the Super Bowl again, this time against the Dallas Cowboys. Unitas, who had led the team there, got hurt in the second quarter; the quarterback who had tried to rally the Colts two years before against the Jets in the Super Bowl, would watch the rest of the game from the bench. Morrall replaced Unitas.

The Colts, who trailed 13-6 at halftime, tied the game in the fourth quarter. Then it was Mike Curtis's turn to be a hero. With less than two minutes remaining, Dallas quarterback Craig Morton tried to move his team for the

Like Curtis, Duane Bickett was an outstanding linebacker.

*Tough guy Bubba
Smith was selected
as an All-Pro for his
outstanding play at
defensive end.*

winning score, but Curtis had other ideas. Morton rolled out to the right and threw downfield; the ball was tipped, and Curtis ripped it out of the air. He returned it to the Dallas 28-yard line. Three plays later Jim O'Brien kicked the game-winning field goal, and the Colts won 16-13. They had claimed their third world championship.

In 1971, the Colts believed they had an even better team. Curtis, who had moved to middle linebacker, was having a great year. He dominated the field, no matter who tried to invade his territory. In one game that season, a spectator ran on the field between plays and tried to steal the ball. Curtis saw the fan and tackled him just as he grabbed the ball.

"Did you see that, did you see those instincts?" said an amazed Bill Curry, the Colts center. "Everybody else was just standing around, but Mike reacted purely on instinct. I felt like telling that fan, that's what I have to face in practice every day."

To Curtis, tackling the fan was nothing special. "My only thought was, this man is interrupting the game—my game," he said. "He had no right to do that. I couldn't let him make fun of the game like that."

Curtis was the key man in a nasty Baltimore defense that also included huge defensive lineman Bubba Smith, linebacker Rudy May, and safeties Rick Volk and Jerry Logan. The Colts, who were now playing in the Eastern Division of the American Football Conference, didn't win their division in 1971. (The American Football League and the National Football League merged in 1970. The Colts were one of the three teams shifted to the new American Football Conference from the NFL.) The Colts did, however, make the playoffs. But Miami, coached by former Colt head man Don Shula, defeated Baltimore 21-0. Miami advanced to the Super Bowl, while the Colts headed home.

As the 1972 season began, the Colts faced a rebuilding project. The team had gotten old, and some of the familiar faces weren't around anymore. In addition, the Colts had a new owner. Carroll Rosenbloom had owned the Colts since 1953, but in 1972, Rosenbloom actually traded the Colts for the Los Angeles Rams, who had just been bought by Robert Irsay. Irsay was the Colts' new owner. The team also had a new general manager; Joe Thomas, who had engineered the trade of the Rams and the Colts, replaced Don Klosterman, who joined Rosenbloom and the Rams.

Rosenbloom and Klosterman had built the Colts into a powerhouse, but they were gone. Soon, so was Unitas, who was traded to San Diego after the 1972 season. Johnny Unitas's reign in Baltimore had ended. When he left Baltimore, he held the all-time records for most pass attempts, most pass completions, most yards passing, and most touchdown passes. To this day, even though almost all of his records have been broken, Unitas is still considered one of the top quarterbacks in NFL history.

The Colts finished 5-9 in 1972, and the fans in Baltimore blamed Thomas for the team's sudden decline. When Thomas traded Unitas, the fans wanted the general manager's scalp. But Thomas was more interested in finding a new quarterback.

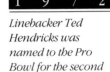

Linebacker Ted Hendricks was named to the Pro Bowl for the second straight season.

JONES JAZZES UP THE COLTS

Thomas knew who he wanted: Louisiana State University quarterback Bert Jones, who had been around pro football all his life. Jones's father, Dub, played and coached

*Running back
Lydell Mitchell was
the club's rushing
leader with over 900
yards gained for the
season.*

with the Cleveland Browns during the 1950s and 1960s. "I grew up around the Browns," Bert Jones remembered. "When I was in high school, I was ballboy for four years at their camp." Dub Jones, a great player himself, knew his son had special abilities. "Best dang rock thrower in Lincoln County," Dub said of his son. "And if you can fling a rock real good, you can fling anything."

Jones was the Colts' first-round draft pick in 1973. The young quarterback spent most of his time on the bench as Baltimore posted records of 4-10 in 1973 and 2-12 in 1974. Thomas, who took over the coaching duties as well in 1974 when he fired Howard Schnellenberger, knew the team needed a change, so he hired an offense-minded coach, Ted Marchibroda. It was the best thing that could have happened as far as Jones was concerned. Marchibroda was a former quarterback who knew the position as well as anyone, and he knew Bert Jones was the secret to Baltimore's success.

"Ted did a mental job on me," Jones said. "We studied films, playbooks, theory, the whole thing. We even graded the other clubs we'd be playing and figured how we might attack them."

When the 1975 season began, Jones was the Colts' starter. Baltimore won its first game, but then lost four in a row. In the next game, the Colts trailed the New York Jets 21-0 at halftime. Baltimore fans screamed for a new quarterback, but Marchibroda was determined to stick with Jones. His decision paid off: Jones and the Colts scored up six touchdowns in the second half and won 45-28. "This may have been the greatest victory I've ever been involved in," Marchibroda rejoiced. But it was only the beginning.

The Colts just kept on winning and winning. In the final two games of the regular season, Jones engineered comeback victories over Miami and New England. The Colts, who had started the season with a 1-4 record, won nine in a row to finish 10-4 and claim the team's first division title in five years. Although Baltimore lost to Pittsburgh in the first round of the playoffs, the future looked very bright. In addition to Jones, the Colts had stars in running back Lydell Mitchell, tight end Raymond Chester, and receivers Glenn Doughty and Freddie Scott. The defense was anchored by a ferocious line—Joe Ehrmann, Mike Barnes, John Dutton, and Fred Cook. Together, they were known as the "Sack Pack," because of their ability to rush the passer. Huge linebacker Ten Hendricks, all six feet seven inches of him, terrorized offenses with his height and long arms.

Quarterback Bert Jones led the Colts to their second straight AFC Eastern Division championship.

Despite all their talent, the Colts struggled during the 1976 preseason, losing four of six games. Owner Robert Irsay fired Marchibroda, but Jones wouldn't stand for that. Jones told Irsay that if Marchibroda wasn't rehired, Jones would leave the team at the end of the 1976 season. Irsay rehired Marchibroda. "I like to look at the bright side of things, and I think that what happened was a blessing because it re-established team unity," Jones reflected. "You know, it takes three mules pulling in the same direction to have a winning football team."

Jones's leadership inspired respect from his teammates. Before a game in 1976 against the Houston Oilers, Jones had a bad case of the flu. But he played anyway, and he led the Colts to victory. "He was so sick yesterday that I thought he'd fall down if an Oiler so much as breathed on him," said offensive lineman George Kunz the next day.

An "Indianapolis" Colt—punter Rohn Stark.

"But he played another great game. He's heady, he's tough, he's wild. It kind of rubs off on the rest of us. And you know what? I've been around this league for eight years, six with Atlanta, and then here, and I've never met a nicer guy at any position. That's why we take care of him."

Together, Jones and the Colts took care of winning. They won the AFC East in 1976 and 1977, but lost in the first round of the playoffs both times. Jones, Lydell Mitchell, and receiver Roger Carr were the stars for the Colts, who were among the most exciting teams in the NFL. But the winning ways didn't last. Mitchell was traded to San Diego in 1978, and Jones started having trouble with injuries. Marchibroda was fired after the 1979 season. The Colts had risen to the top very quickly under Jones; unfortunately, they fell just as quickly to the bottom. Once last place became a reality, the Colts decided to build for the future, so they traded Jones to the Los Angeles Rams in 1981.

The "Baltimore" Colts never had another winning season, and they became one of the worst teams in the league. After the team went 7-9 in 1983, Irsay decided he had had enough of Baltimore. At first, he thought about moving the team to Phoenix, but a group from Indianapolis talked Irsay into moving the team to that city. It wasn't a tough sell. Indianapolis had just finished building the sixty-thousand-seat Hoosier Dome, a beautiful indoor stadium.

The Colts had a new home, but they were still losers. Frank Kush, a defense-minded coach, was replaced by Rod Dowhower, an offensive genius. The new coach didn't change the team's luck. The Colts had some good players, such as running backs Curtis Dickey and Randy McMillan,

1 9 7 9

Running back Joe Washington led the NFL with eighty-two pass receptions.

23

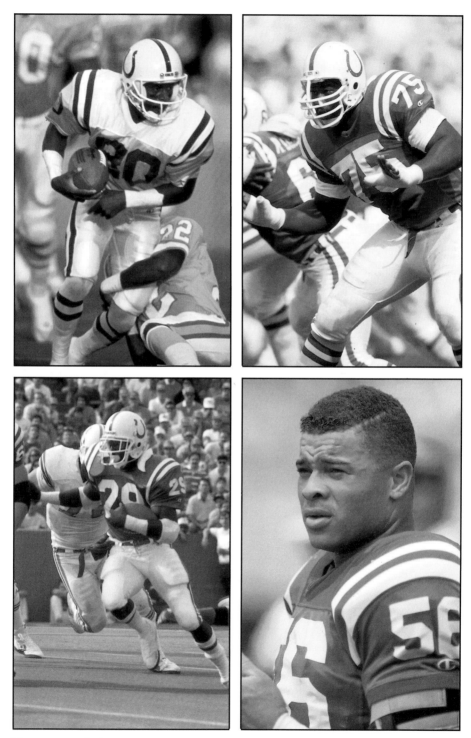

Clockwise: Bill Brooks, Chris Hinton, Fredd Young, Eric Dickerson.

linebacker Barry Krauss, cornerback Eugene Daniel, and safety Nesby Glasgow, but the team didn't have enough talent to compete. In 1986 Indianapolis lost its first thirteen games. General manager Jim Irsay, son of the owner, fired Dowhower and named Ron Meyer as the new coach. Meyer had an immediate impact, as the Colts won their last three games of 1986. Suddenly, hopes were high for 1987.

1 9 8 7

Eric Dickerson blazed for over a thousand yards, despite joining the team halfway through the season.

DICKERSON RUNS TO INDIANAPOLIS

The Colts were an improved team in 1987, but Irsay found a way to make the team much better with just one player. He wasn't just any player, though: he was the best running back in the NFL.

No runner had as quick a rise to the top as Eric Dickerson. Drafted by the Los Angeles Rams in 1983, Dickerson led the NFL in rushing his rookie year. He was the main weapon in the Rams' offense; sometimes he was the only weapon. By 1987, though, Dickerson no longer wanted to play for Los Angeles. He felt he should be paid more, but the Rams refused to rewrite his contract. Finally, Dickerson told the Rams to trade him.

Jim Irsay knew Dickerson was unhappy in Los Angeles. He called Meyer and asked, "Do you want to take a run at getting Eric Dickerson?" "I love it!" Meyer exclaimed.

The trade was finally made in early November 1987. In Dickerson, the Colts had their first superstar since Bert Jones. "When we first heard about the trade," said Colts' quarterback Jack Trudeau, "we were saying, 'Can you imagine Eric Dickerson in a Colts' uniform?' No one could."

Running back Albert Bentley, (pages 26–27).

For the second consecutive year, Eric Dickerson (right) led the Colts in rushing and was named All-Pro.

But Dickerson was a Colt. He was also something special. Sometimes Dickerson even shocked himself with his abilities. One day in 1987, he was recalling a run he made while in college at Southern Methodist University. "I ran up in the hole, stopped, jumped back, and ran the other way," Dickerson remembered. "It was one of the most amazing moves I've ever seen, but when I saw the film, it was like I was watching another guy do it."

Dickerson ran so smoothly that people thought he was just coasting, not running as hard as he could. During Dickerson's rookie year with the Rams, Los Angeles coach John Robinson kept yelling at Dickerson, "You've got to run faster, Eric. You've got to run faster."

"Coach," Dickerson said, "come out and run with me. I'm running as fast as I can."

When Dickerson joined the Colts, Meyer already had the team believing it could win. Running back Albert Bentley was a solid runner and pass catcher, and receiver Bill Brooks was a deep threat. But the best part of the Colts' offense was the line: center Ray Donaldson, guard Ron Solt, and tackle Chris Hinton were all Pro Bowl-quality players. Dickerson and Bentley both had success running behind this trio. On defense, linebacker Duane Bickett led the team in sacks, but he also could stop the run and defend against the pass downfield. Bickett, like the offensive linemen, was a Pro Bowl pick.

1 9 9 0

Left tackle Chris Hinton was one of several players traded to Atlanta for quarterback Jeff George.

All of this talent combined to lead the Colts to a 9-6 record in 1987, which was good enough to win the AFC Eastern Division title. The Colts had made it to the playoffs for the first time in ten years, but they lost in the first round to Cleveland. However, it was obvious that the Colts were now contenders.

In 1988, Indianapolis made two key additions. The team obtained linebacker Fredd Young in a trade with the Seattle Seahawks and drafted a quarterback, Chris Chandler, who had an immediate impact as a rookie. Chandler beat out veterans Jack Trudeau and Gary Hogeboom for the job and led the team to a 9-7 record. Unfortunately, that wasn't good enough to qualify for postseason play. The following year, injuries sidelined Chandler for almost all of the season and Dickerson for part of it. Trudeau filled in for Chandler, but he couldn't lead the hurting Colts to the playoffs.

Despite falling short of postseason play recently, the Colts are confident they are building toward a Super Bowl championship. In the 1990 NFL college draft, the Colts traded promising players Chris Hinton and wide receiver

Fredd Young (#56) came to Indianapolis via the Seattle Seahawks.

The one and only Eric Dickerson.

Andre Rison, as well as draft choices, to the Atlanta Falcons for the top pick in the draft. The Colts then selected University of Illinois quarterback Jeff George and signed him to a $15 million contract.

Indianapolis coaches believe George is the key to returning the team to a championship status. The fans in Indianapolis have never had a chance to cheer for an NFL title winner. But the Colts franchise has known such success before. The Baltimore Colts were one of the best teams in pro football from the late 1950s to the early 1970s. The Indianapolis Colts are now hopeful they can repeat those glory days in the 1990s.